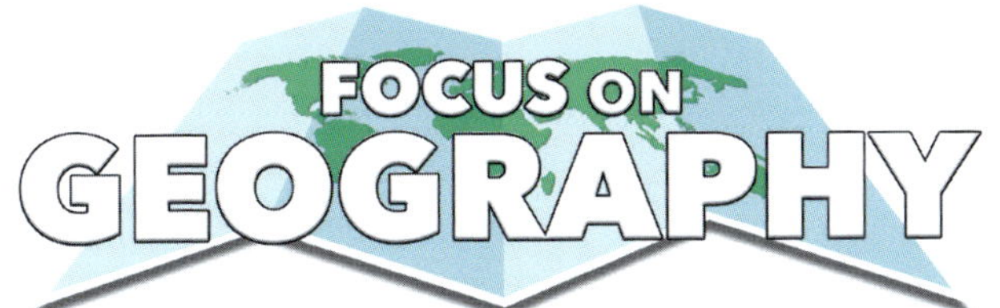

Focus on Switzerland

Linda Barghoorn

A Crabtree Forest Book

Crabtree Publishing
crabtreebooks.com

Author: Linda Barghoorn

Series research and development: Janine Deschenes

Editorial director: Kathy Middleton

Editor: Janine Deschenes

Proofreader: Melissa Boyce

Design: Tammy McGarr

IMAGE CREDITS

Alamy: Emma Wood, p 25 (top left); Dorling Kindersley ltd, p 26 (top)

Lötschental Marketing AG, p 39 (top)

Shutterstock: saiko3p, front cover (top left); Fedor Selivanov, p 3; marekusz p 5 (bottom right); olrat, p 7 (bottom left); PixHound p 14 (top); Capricorn Studio p 18; Jakub Korczyk Services p 19 (top), p 21 (top); Suteren, p 20 (bottom); Michael Derrer Fuchs p 21 (bottom left); Longfin Media p 23 (bottom); Stefano Ember, p 24, p 42 (top); Michael Derrer Fuchs, p 26 (bottom); Roman Babakin p 27 (top); Benny Marty, p 28 (bottom); yangjlin p 28 (top inset); S-Studio p 29 (middle); 2p2play p 29 (bottom); Daily Travel Photos p 29 (top); Arsenie Krasnevsky, p 32 (top); Yamagiwa, p 34; George Paolo Silva Mota, p 35 (top); Stefano Ember, p 36; Andrii Shepeliev, p 37 (bottom); Tapati Rinchumrus, p 39 (bottom); Ceri Breeze, p 42 (bottom); Thitichaya Somdulyawad, p 44 (bottom)

Wikimedia Commons: Capricorn4049, p 11 (bottom); Paebi, p 25 (top right); Michał Rawlik, p 32 (bottom); Museo nazionale del Risorgimento, Torino, p 33 (bottom); Henry_Dunant-young, p 33 (top)

Crabtree Publishing

crabtreebooks.com **800-387-7650**

In Canada: We acknowledge the financial support of the Government of Canada through the Canada Book Fund for our publishing activities.

Hardcover 978-1-0398-1524-7
Paperback 978-1-0398-1550-6
Ebook (pdf) 978-1-0398-1602-2
Epub 978-1-0398-1576-6

Published in Canada
Crabtree Publishing
616 Welland Avenue
St. Catharines, Ontario
L2M 5V6

Published in the United States
Crabtree Publishing
347 Fifth Avenue
Suite 1402-145
New York, New York, 10016

Library and Archives Canada Cataloguing in Publication
Available at Library and Archives Canada

Library of Congress Cataloging-in-Publication Data
Available at the Library of Congress

Printed in the U.S.A./072023/CG20230214

Contents

Introduction

Snapshot of Life in Bern

With a population of just 133,000, residents of the historic city of Bern, Switzerland's capital, enjoy the small-town feel of their city. Its narrow, twisting alleyways and **medieval** architecture reflect its ancient heritage. Since it was founded more than 900 years ago, it has grown into a bustling, prosperous 21st-century city. A distinctly multicultural city, it is influenced by the cultures and countries that surround it. But its people also take great pride in its deeply rooted traditions, culture, languages, and history.

Built on a narrow hillside where the river curves, Bern's streets and buildings are packed tightly together. Eventually more bridges were built, allowing the city to expand across the river. While the newer city is more modern, the Old City remains much as it did centuries ago.

Bern's location on the gentle hills and **fertile** meadows of the Swiss **plateau**—between the Jura and Alps mountain ranges—was ideally suited to agriculture. Today, one in five farms in Switzerland are in the **canton** of Bern. Weekly farmers' markets offer Bern's citizens a rich selection of the region's agricultural products—from fresh produce to cheese, meat, and honey.

As Switzerland modernized in the 19th century, its cities grew as **commercial** and **industrial** hubs. Bern became an important center for the production of chemical and **pharmaceutical** products and machinery. The chocolate industry also thrives in Bern, where every Toblerone chocolate bar sold around the world is made. The Swiss consume more chocolate per person than any other country in the world!

Outdoor activities are a big part of life in the canton of Bern. People enjoy swimming and rafting in the Aare River, hiking and biking in the area's varied terrain, and skiing and snowshoeing in the winter months.

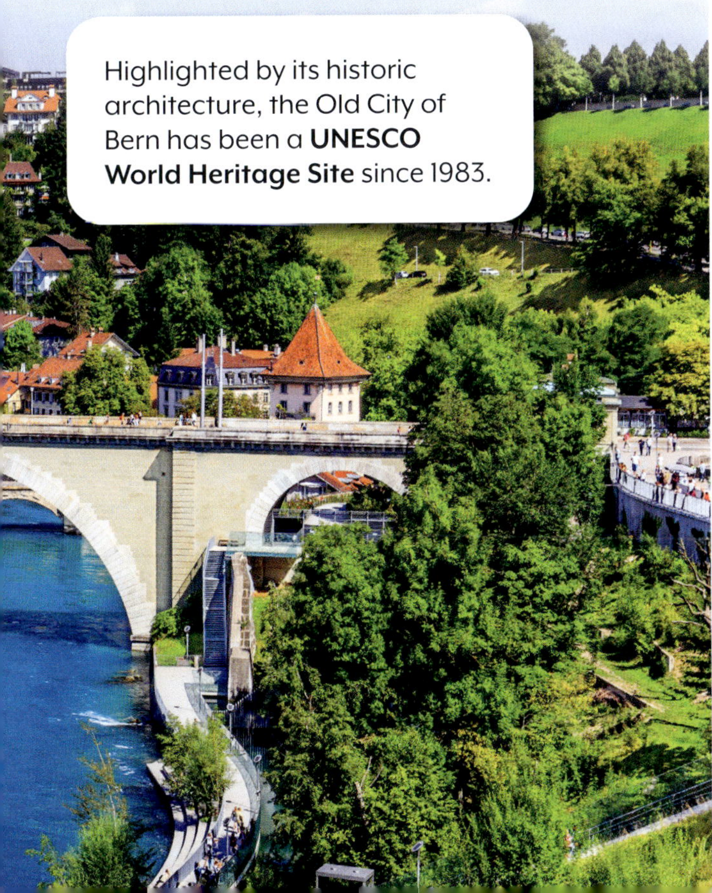

Highlighted by its historic architecture, the Old City of Bern has been a **UNESCO World Heritage Site** since 1983.

Legend says that Duke Berchtold V, who founded Bern, named the city after the first animal he met on a hunt there: a bear.

The Alps cover about 65 percent of Switzerland's land area.

Introducing Switzerland

Switzerland is a **landlocked** country located at the center of Europe. It is famous for its incredible natural beauty, from rugged snow-capped mountains to lush, green valleys. Dotted across these landscapes are **quaint** villages and farms that have been passed down through generations of families.

Several major rivers, including the Rhine, trace their sources to Switzerland. They are critical sources of water for much of Europe. The Alps mountain range dominates the country's southern regions and contains the highest peaks on the continent. It attracts hikers, climbers, skiers, photographers, and tourists from around the world.

Many of Switzerland's cities have cultures and styles that are a wonderful blend of medieval and modern. Some—including Geneva, Basel, Zürich, and Bern—were established on one of the country's many lakes and rivers, which served as important transportation and trade routes. Today these cities are important international centers of trade, finance, fashion, and industry.

Switzerland's population today is less than 9 million people—quite small compared to many of its European neighbors. But its **population density** is among the highest, with most of its people stretched across a thin belt of fertile prairie known as the *Mittelland*, or "middle country." The Alps mountain range is largely **inhospitable** to human settlement.

Switzerland is bordered by France, Germany, Austria, Liechtenstein, and Italy. Each of these countries has had an incredible influence on Swiss traditions, culture, food, and languages. Switzerland is a distinctly multilingual, multicultural country. Its constitution recognizes four official languages: French, German, Italian, and Romansh. Left by the Roman Celts almost 2,000 years ago, Romansh is a dying language—spoken by very few people today. As the language is being lost, local cultures and traditions are being lost along with it.

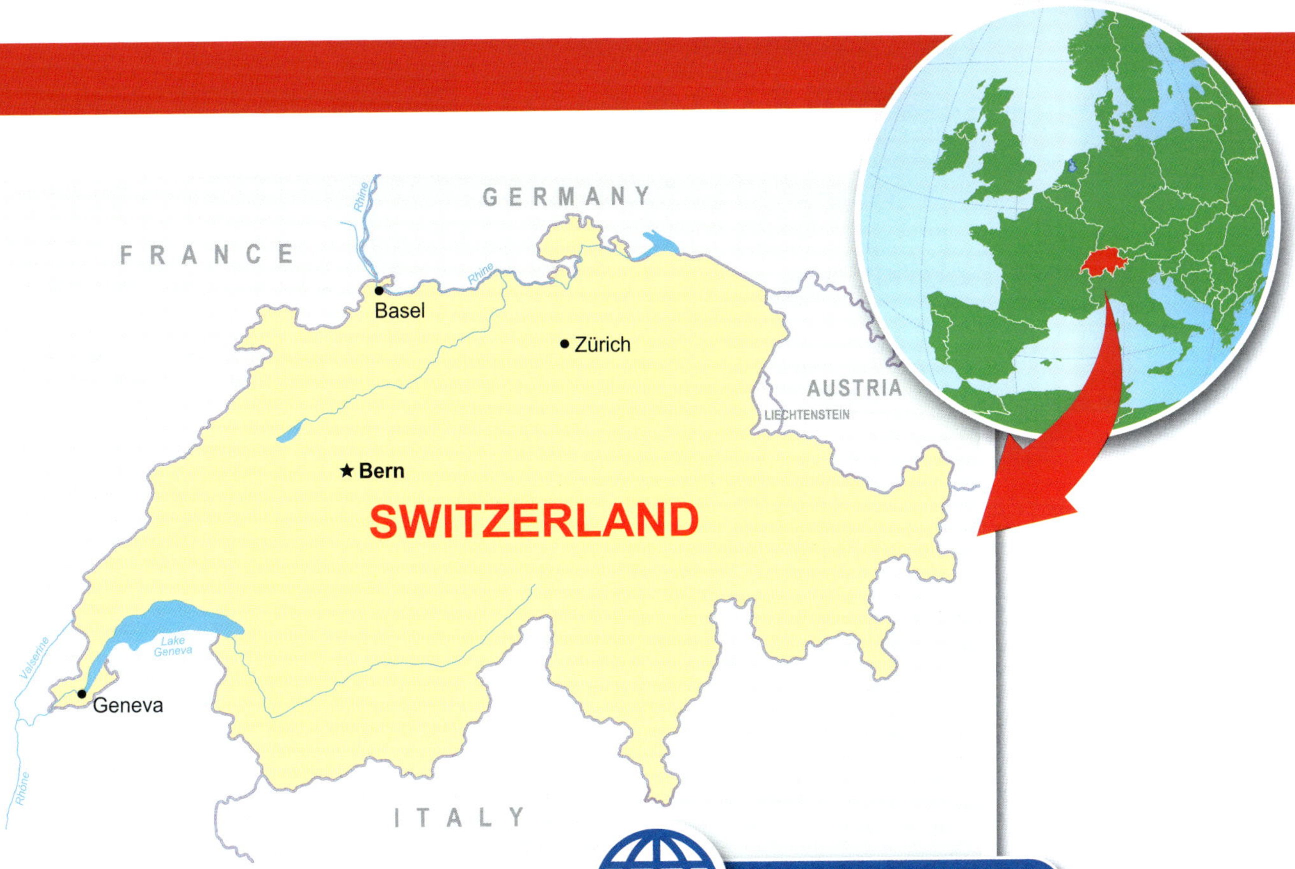

GERMANY
FRANCE
Rhine
Basel
Zürich
AUSTRIA
LIECHTENSTEIN
★ Bern
SWITZERLAND
Lake Geneva
Valserine
Geneva
Rhône
ITALY

Many international organizations, such as the United Nations, the World Health Organization, and the Red Cross, have their headquarters in Geneva. This makes the city an important center for **diplomacy**.

AT A GLANCE

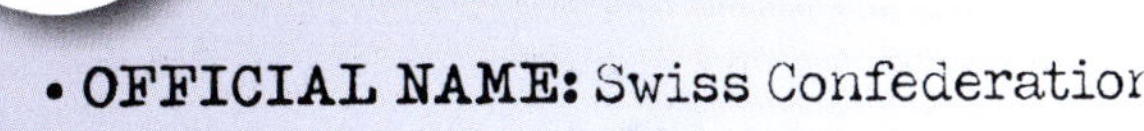

- **OFFICIAL NAME:** Swiss Confederation
- **NATIONAL CAPITAL:** Bern
- **POPULATION:** 8,771,000
- **OFFICIAL LANGUAGES:** French, German, Italian, Romansh
- **LAND AREA:** 15,940 square miles (41,285 sq. km)

CHAPTER 1

The Land

Physical Geography

Switzerland stretches just 135 miles (220 km) from north to south and 220 miles (350 km) from west to east. Three geographically distinct regions characterize the country.

The Jura mountain range—in the northwest—makes up about 10 percent of Switzerland's area. Its name comes from the Celtic word for "forest." These mountains were formed during the same period as the mighty Alps. But their peaks are covered with alpine meadows and **sparse** forests rather than snow and ice. Their valleys also provided easy transportation for early settlers. For this reason, the Jura were not a significant barrier to the movement of people in and across Switzerland.

The Alps—in the south and east—are much higher and cover more than half of Switzerland's land mass. The highest peak is the Dufourspitze at 15,203 feet (4,634 m), but the Matterhorn peak is the most famous. This mountain range is the **watershed** for much of Europe. Three important rivers have their sources there: the Rhine, the Rhône, and the Po. Rocky and snow-covered, the Alps are a rather inhospitable place for large-scale human settlement, which has been mostly limited to small villages and resorts.

The Matterhorn—with its distinctive pyramid shape—has become an important symbol of Switzerland.

The Mittelland is a long plateau which stretches between the two mountain ranges and covers about one-third of the country. It is bordered by Switzerland's two largest lakes: Lake Geneva on the western border and Lake Constance to the east. Its fertile meadows make it much more suited to human settlement. It has become both the agricultural heartland of the country and the site of most Swiss cities. It is highly **urbanized** and **industrialized**.

The Mittelland is home to about two-thirds of Switzerland's population. It is the most densely populated area in the country, and includes cities such as Lucerne (below).

Climate and Weather

The Alps mountain range plays an enormous role in shaping Switzerland's climate. It acts as a giant weather barrier to create a variety of regional conditions. Oceanic **currents** bring warm, moist air from the Atlantic Ocean and Mediterranean Sea, which **moderates** winter and summer temperatures across the southern and western regions of the country. Continental currents, which travel across Asia, bring dry, cold air in the winter and warm air in the summer to eastern regions. The climate across the Mittelland plateau is the most temperate, making it well-suited for human settlement.

Foehn winds are a unique characteristic of Switzerland. Air currents climb up one side of a mountain, cross its peak, and then descend on the other side. As they descend, they gather speed, causing sudden and dramatic temperature increases—sometimes by as much as 25 degrees Fahrenheit (14 degrees Celsius) in just a few hours. This can cause the top layers of snow on the sheltered side of the mountain to warm quickly and melt. Avalanches can result from these conditions. People who live in mountain villages plan ahead to protect themselves from these destructive weather events.

Much of the country is blanketed in thick layers of snow during the winter.

Because of the region's favorable climate and fertile land, about half of the land in the Mittelland is used for farming.

Closer Look

Alpine cantons have about 10,000 avalanches every year. Most are between February and April.

Avalanche Awareness

An avalanche is a large, fast-moving shelf of snow that collapses from a mountainside and races down its slope. Avalanches can move huge boulders and uproot trees. This can make way for new plant life to take root, providing food sources for animals. But avalanches can also block transportation routes and destroy homes, roads, bridges, and towns. They can be deadly to people and animals that live on the mountainsides. Switzerland has centuries of experience in dealing with deadly avalanches. The country has developed an advanced warning system and readiness training to deal with the effects of an avalanche. Snow conditions are monitored and published regularly to warn people of danger. Infrastructure—like steel bridges and snow nets—has been developed to limit the destructive forces of an avalanche. The country also takes emergency measures such as closing roads and evacuating communities at risk.

Researchers can measure snow stability to identify at-risk areas so better preparation and response measures can be planned.

The ibex, a mountain goat, thrives in the Alps. These herbivores graze mostly on grasses but also eat moss, flowers, and leaves.

Wildlife and Natural Resources

A number of wildlife species, such as the ibex and bearded vulture, are particularly suited to Switzerland's rugged mountain geography. In recent centuries, others, including the lynx and brown bear, have been devastated by pollution, overhunting, and human expansion. The lynx has been reintroduced to the country, while wolves and bears have migrated back from neighboring countries. While their populations are expanding, their existence remains fragile.

Lower elevations typically feature **deciduous** trees, which change to **conifers** as elevations increase. Between the tree line and the permanent snow line, grassy meadows and alpine vegetation dominate. These meadows are ideal for raising cattle. Sheep and cows graze there during the summer and are brought down to the valleys during the cold winters. Global warming is having an impact on vegetation, however. As temperatures rise, plants are growing at higher altitudes up the mountains.

Switzerland has few natural mineral resources. The only mined resource is salt, left behind from a shallow sea millions of years ago. The country's biggest natural asset is water, which flows into many neighboring countries. Many rivers are controlled by enormous dams, which generate hydroelectric power.

The amount of **arable** land is limited by the country's mountainous **topography**. Forests cover about one-third of the country and are carefully protected and managed. Much of the arable land available is suitable only as grasslands—used for grazing animals—because of the harsh geography and climate. Farmers in the Mittelland grow grains, cereals, fruits, and vegetables.

Researchers have found that due to global warming, animals such as the ibex and red deer are spending more time at higher elevations where their food sources now grow.

The Rhône Valley, irrigated by the Rhône River, is known for the fruits and vegetables grown there. Vineyards can also be found on its sunny hillsides.

Early Settlement

Switzerland's rugged physical geography played an enormous role in the way humans migrated and settled in Switzerland and across Europe. The towering Alps mountain range acted like a huge roadblock that stretched across Switzerland. Historically, just a few mountain passages provided access from northern to southern Europe. Around 50,000 years ago, early **Neanderthals** established hunting settlements in Switzerland. **Nomadic** hunters used caves in the Jura Mountains and Mittelland plateau as their camps. From these caves, they set out in search of reindeer and bears.

Around 7,000 years ago, people established agricultural settlements to grow corn and raise livestock. Three thousand years later, Bronze Age settlements spread across these regions. One of the oldest was Chur, located at a strategic junction of the Rhine River and a mountain pass. Celtic tribes then arrived in Switzerland around 2,000 years ago. They took control of much of the region between the Jura and Alps mountain ranges. The Helvetians were the largest of these tribes.

The Bronze Age (3000 to 1000 B.C.E.) marks the first time people began working with metals to create goods such as these pots and containers.

Chur is the oldest city in Switzerland, dating back more than 2,500 years.

Closer Look

La Tène

Much of what we know today about Celtic culture has been learned from the archaeological site at La Tène, established on the shores of Lake Neuchâtel, Switzerland, around 450 B.C.E. As the Celts spread across central Europe, Celtic traders and warriors had frequent contact with the Greek and Roman civilizations that ruled southern Europe. These trading partners had strong influences on the Celts. They developed sophisticated ironworking skills and learned to build chariots that improved upon the ancient Roman design. Most inhabitants of La Tène were farmers. They developed new agricultural methods, including a heavy-wheeled iron plow. Eventually the Celtic civilization was destroyed by the Romans. The only evidence of this culture's rich heritage is found in the archaeological site that remains. Today La Tène is a quiet resort village on the shores of beautiful Lake Neuchâtel.

Many elements of modern Swiss culture, including its currency, reflect its Celtic past.

Switzerland's Celtic roots live on in such towns as Thun, in the canton of Bern.

Many Celtic artifacts were discovered at La Tène when the shoreline of Lake Neuchâtel dropped to an unusually low level.

CHAPTER 2

Becoming Switzerland

Celts, Romans, and Germans

The Celts traded among themselves and with the Greek and Roman civilizations in southern Europe. They learned valuable skills from the Greeks and Romans, including agriculture, craftsmanship, and warfare. They used these skills to develop new tools. Iron axes allowed them to clear forests to create more arable land. An iron plow enabled them to farm more productively. As their population grew, they expanded across the Mittelland and built larger settlements. Often these were along lakes, rivers, or mountain passes, which enabled transportation of people and goods.

When the Celts attempted to move farther south in 58 B.C.E., they were pushed back by the Roman army. Decades later, the Roman Emperor invaded and conquered the Celtic territories. The Romans expanded roads and mountain passes to connect important trading cities—like Geneva, Basel, and Zürich—with their administrative center in Rome. They **fortified** farmsteads and introduced new fruits, vegetables, and grapevines to produce wine. Many of these agricultural products were transported to the Roman Empire farther south.

The Romans also introduced Christianity to the region. The majority of people living in Switzerland today are Christian.

Some of the regions controlled by Germanic tribes became the basis for Switzerland's regional territories, called cantons.

As the Roman Empire began to decline, Germanic tribes—eager to control the **profitable** trade routes—invaded. By 400 C.E., they occupied much of the region. Each brought their own language and culture. As these tribes continued to push farther up the Rhine Valley, the Celts were forced deeper into the Alps. Today the descendants of the Celts include the few Swiss people who continue to speak Romansh, the ancient language of the Celtic tribes.

In 800 C.E., the region became part of the Holy Roman Empire of Charlemagne, who ruled over much of western Europe. Switzerland was at the heart of this territory and held many strategic transportation routes and trading cities.

Visitors can immerse themselves in Roman history at the Augusta Raurica archaeological site and museum in northern Switzerland.

Feudal Dynasties and the Creation of the Swiss Confederation

Emperor Charlemagne controlled a network of noble families whose dukes, princes, and kings were in constant competition for his attention and favor. These **feudal** dynasties—led by powerful families like the Savoys, the Habsburgs, and the Kingdom of Burgundy—competed with one another for the power and wealth that came with control of the land and its trade routes.

In 1291, the Swiss Confederation was created when three ruling families—the Uri, Schwyz, and Unterwalden—formed an alliance against the Habsburg dynasty that ruled over much of the region. The goal of this alliance was to control the Gotthard route—a key passage through the Alps that linked northern and southern Europe. This would allow them to **consolidate** power and control trade. They also hoped an alliance would bring peace and stability to the region. The alliance was signed on August 1, 1291.

To commemorate the creation of the Swiss Confederation, August 1 is celebrated each year as Swiss National Day.

Visitors to Switzerland can take a unique train and boat trip along the Gotthard route.

Switzerland is still known for its neutrality—a position that was officially adopted into the country's politics.

Each of these families ruled over a canton—a territory that acted like an independent state, responsible for its own borders, army, and currency. Strategically located towns—like Bern, Zug, Lucerne, and Zürich—later joined the Confederation. They became important trade and transportation hubs as Swiss traders traveled farther to cities across Europe. Rural and urban communities united in a common purpose of trade and defense against threats of foreign invasions.

The Swiss Confederation remained mostly **neutral**, even as war continued to rage across much of Europe. This neutrality allowed the country to prosper as a peaceful and reliable trading partner with other countries. By the time it became an official nation in 1848, it had grown to 22 cantons, each with its own unique set of languages, culture, and traditions.

Industry, Trade, and Transport

At the geographic crossroads of Europe, Switzerland prospered as an important trade hub. In the 15th century, Geneva became a key import center for raw cotton and finished **textiles** from Asia. Later, religious refugees fleeing France brought their textile and watchmaking skills to Geneva. Bankers also profited by financing warring armies across Europe.

In order to support a growing population and economy, Switzerland began to industrialize in the 18th century. Basel became an important center for chemical and pharmaceutical industries. Early chemical factories produced dyes for the textile industry. Later they expanded to produce vaccines and drugs. By the mid 19th century, Switzerland had become one of the most industrialized countries in Europe.

There are more than 1,000 tunnels in Switzerland, with more being built to allow for easier transportation routes through the mountainous country.

Tunnels were the best means to improve transportation through Switzerland's mountainous terrain. The first alpine tunnel was constructed in 1707. By the 20th century, an intricate web of tunnels had been built to allow the flow of goods and people from across Europe through Switzerland.

In 2020, Switzerland was the second-largest exporter of pharmaceutical products in the world.

Closer Look

St. Gotthard Pass

The St. Gotthard Pass is steeped in history and legend. For centuries, the passageway provided a somewhat treacherous route through the rocky, high-altitude, snow-covered Alps. During the Roman occupation, it was a simple stone pathway passable only on foot or with mules. Even as it was improved in later centuries, snow often made it impassable for months at a time. The first railway tunnel along the route was opened in 1882. A highway tunnel followed 100 years later. Finally, in 2016, a high-speed rail tunnel—the longest on Earth—was opened. Called the Gotthard Base Tunnel (GBT), it is 35.5 miles (57 km) long—an engineering masterpiece cut deep into the mountains.

The Gotthard Base Tunnel increases **freight** transportation and helps reduce pollution caused by large trucks. It also helps travelers move between major cities more quickly.

The tunnel passes by the "Devil's Bridge," which crosses the Schöllenen Gorge. It was named after a legend which tells the story of a bargain with the devil that allowed the successful building of the bridge.

Cultural Influences

Because of its location, Switzerland has been deeply influenced by its neighbors—especially France, Germany, and Italy. They have shaped Switzerland's regional cultures, languages, foods, and identities. For example, the city of Ticino, which is in the south, has been shaped by Italy, while Geneva has been shaped by France, and Zürich has been shaped by Germany.

The country's political structure now includes 26 regional cantons. Cultural differences have evolved to reflect Switzerland's different geographies—from rural mountain communities to the towns and cities of Switzerland's central plateau. Switzerland's diverse foods, languages, and clothing reflect the different traditions of these regions.

In rural regions, clothing tends to be simple and functional, while in urban centers it is often more stylish and refined. The national costume reflects the traditional dress worn by people in rural communities. Noble families often wore costumes that mirrored those in neighboring countries. Clothes were made of homespun material: wool in winter and cotton in summer. As the country has modernized, many Swiss have abandoned the traditional costume in favor of modern, international styles. But traditional costumes continue to play an important role in regional and national celebrations.

Men's lederhosen—which originated in Germany—were popular in alpine regions as they are well-suited for climbing or hiking in the mountains.

Often, the color of women's clothing was an indication of where they lived and whether they were married or single. White, for example, represented Obwalden canton, and blue represented Zürich.

SWITZERLAND'S 26 CANTONS

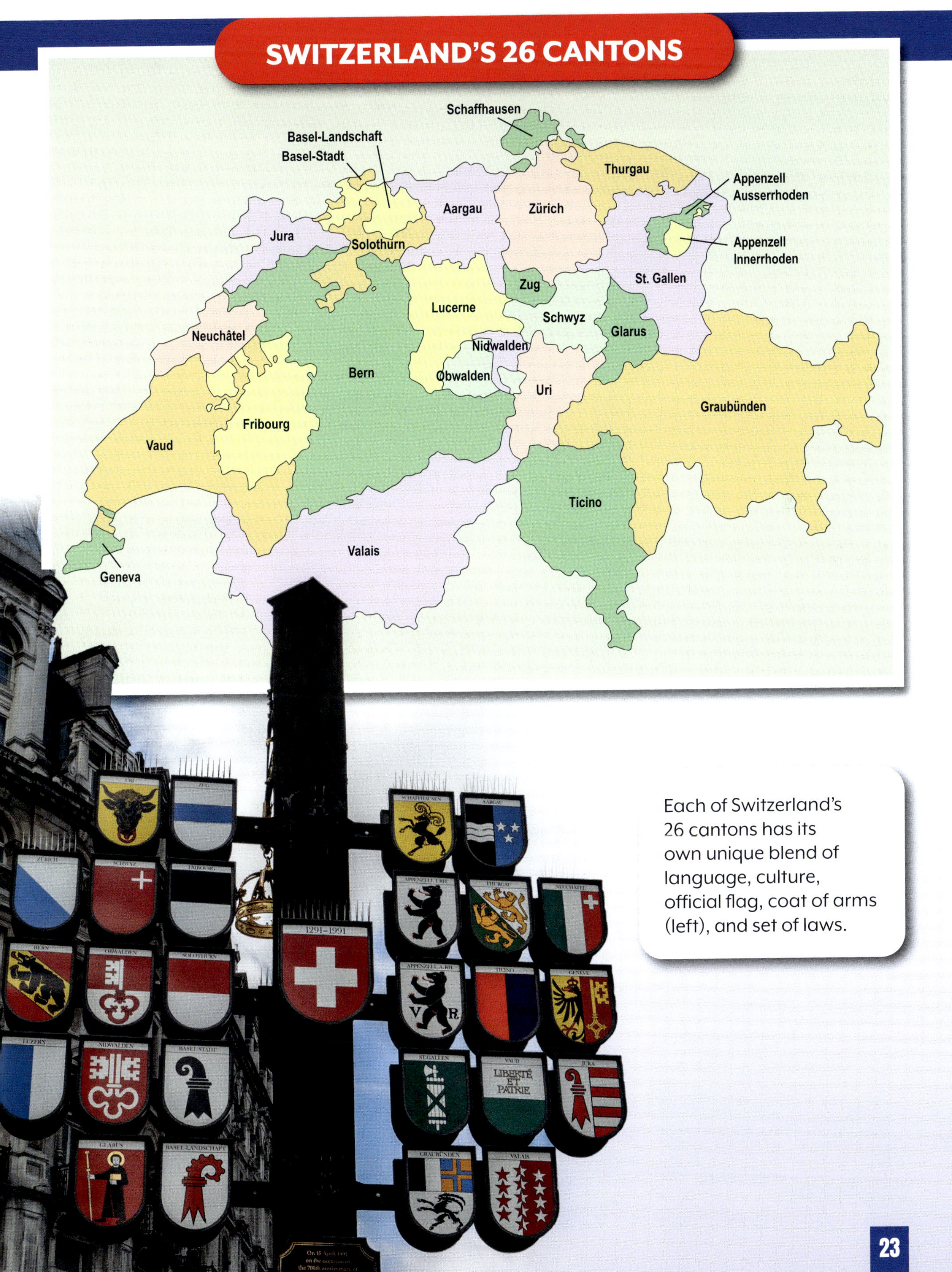

Each of Switzerland's 26 cantons has its own unique blend of language, culture, official flag, coat of arms (left), and set of laws.

CHAPTER 3

Life Today

21st-Century Switzerland

Despite conflicts in its early history, 21st-century Switzerland is an orderly and peaceful place to live. Switzerland has one of the highest standards of living in the world, with excellent medical care and long life expectancies. At the same time, life is extremely expensive in Switzerland. The cost of living there is among the highest in Europe. To help citizens cope, salaries are high and the country's minimum wage is among the highest in the world.

In rural areas, some folk traditions, such as yodeling, are still practiced. Local festivals have taken place for centuries. They may celebrate farming events and religious occasions. Farming, including cattle breeding, is an important part of life in rural Switzerland.

Multiculturalism is an important aspect of Swiss culture. It has a long history in Switzerland's relationship with its neighbors. Swiss people take great pride in this and their reputation as a peaceful, free, multiethnic country. Language reflects their multiculturalism, with about 60 percent of people speaking German, 20 percent speaking French, and around 8 to 10 percent speaking Italian. Only around 1 percent of Swiss people speak Romansh today.

Switzerland's spectacular natural environment is ideal for a wide variety of outdoor sports activities and the Swiss are outdoor enthusiasts. Switzerland is world famous for its majestic landscapes and winter sports, which draw tourists from around the world. Around 20 million people visit the country each year, making it one of the most popular countries on the planet for tourists.

Yodeling is a tradition in European alpine areas and is still a major part of Swiss folk music today.

The *Knabenschiessen* festival, one of the oldest in Switzerland, is held in Zürich in September. Teenagers from across the country compete in archery and other shooting events.

Swiss children often participate in sports at school or in community clubs. Skiing, mountain climbing, hockey, biking, and soccer are popular.

Language and Urban Life

Although the Alps cover about 65 percent of Switzerland's land mass, only about one in 10 people live there. Most people have settled in the Mittelland, where the warmer climate, fertile lands, and well-developed transportation system are more hospitable to human settlement. This region has become the most highly urbanized and industrialized in the country. It includes the major cities of Bern, Geneva, Zürich, and Lausanne.

Graubünden is the only canton where Romansh is an official language.

About 75 percent of Switzerland's population is urban. But in comparison with other major cities around the world, Swiss cities are small. Zürich, the largest, has a population of around 400,000. The amount of land available for human settlement is quite limited. That means land for housing is limited. Most people live in apartments rather than houses. House prices are also quite high, making it difficult for many citizens to own their homes.

Zürich is an important financial center in both Switzerland and Europe. Many banks and large corporations were founded there.

Ascona (above), in the canton of Ticino, is heavily influenced by its proximity to Italy. Most people there are Italian speakers. Similarly, German-speaking cities, such as Basel and Zürich, are closest to Germany in the north. French-speaking Geneva and Lausanne are in the west, closest to France.

Röstigraben

Each of the country's 26 cantons has its own official language. Most often, this language is a reflection of the region's proximity to a neighboring country and its language. German-speaking cantons—there are 17—are the most common. There are four French-speaking cantons and one Italian-speaking canton. Three cantons are bilingual, with official languages of French and German. Graubünden canton, located high in the Alps, is trilingual and the only place where Romansh is still spoken, a tribute to its Celtic past.

Food, culture, and language are intricately woven in Switzerland—so much so that the foods typical of a region have been used to coin terms that refer to the people who live there. *Röstigraben*—named after the popular German *rösti* or potato pancake—is a term used to define the cultural line that divides French and German-speaking parts of Switzerland. *Polentagraben*—named for the popular Italian polenta dish—represents the boundary which separates German-speaking cantons from the Italian-speaking canton of Ticino.

Montreux waterfront at sunset

Tourism is an important industry in Switzerland. The city of Montreux hosts an annual music festival that draws jazz music enthusiasts from around the world.

Industry

The Swiss import most **raw materials**, which they manufacture into high-quality finished products. They are a global leader in **precision machinery**, pharmaceuticals, and chemical manufacturing. A number of global organizations in these industries are based in Switzerland. Many of their products are exported around the world. Enormous investments in research, technology, and training have allowed Switzerland to excel in these industries.

Swiss cities are leading centers of industry and trade. Geneva continues its historic role as an important banking and finance center. It owes its success largely to Switzerland's reputation for stability, privacy, and security, which dates back to the 18th century.

About one-third of the country's land is devoted to agriculture, producing grains, fruits, vegetables, and wine. Cattle raising and dairy are important industries in the Mittelland and low-lying mountain regions. They contribute to products that are exported around the world, including milk, butter, and, of course, the famous Swiss cheese!

Several large companies, such as Nestlé, are based in Switzerland. More than 10,000 Swiss citizens are employed by Nestlé.

Closer Look

Swiss Watchmaking

While Switzerland leads the world in precision watchmaking today, it was not always so. Back in the 16th century, the Germans and French were the most skilled watchmakers in Europe. Most watches were worn like a piece of jewelry and were so expensive that only the very wealthy could afford them. As war broke out in Germany and then France, people fled to Switzerland for safety. Skilled French watchmakers settled in Geneva in the middle of the 16th century. Already a key center for jewelry making and goldsmithing, the city was well suited to encourage a growing watchmaking industry. It remains the **epicenter** of this industry in Switzerland.

Around 60,000 people work in Switzerland's watchmaking industry.

Many watch brands popular today are Swiss, including the luxury brands Rolex and Breitling.

Human Impact on Environment

Climate change is one of the biggest threats to Switzerland's alpine landscapes and its way of life. As global temperatures rise, Switzerland is likely to see its large glaciers shrink and its smaller ones disappear altogether. Fewer days of snowfall are also likely. With higher alpine temperatures, permafrost zones—layers of rock, gravel, and sand bound together by ice on Earth's surface—will begin to thaw. Massive rockslides will become more common as a result. These will threaten wildlife and mountain communities.

Forests cover about one-third of Switzerland. They are critical in helping to protect Switzerland's watersheds, which are important sources of water for human populations and industry. Forests are also extremely effective natural barriers to avalanches. During the last century, air pollution and **acid rain** damaged approximately one-fifth of the country's forests. Communities that rely on forests for avalanche protection will need to develop effective human-made barriers to replace lost areas of forest.

To prevent large avalanches and minimize the risk to communities, artificial avalanches can be planned when snow builds up. This allows professionals to control how the snow moves.

Artificial protective structures, such as metal and concrete netting and barriers, can help protect villages, highways, recreational areas, and alpine paths from avalanches.

Alpine plants will continue to grow in more northern areas as global temperatures increase.

Drier alpine soils have also restricted the ability of trees to produce **resins**, which protect them from destructive insects like the spruce beetle. As trees die, entire forests become drier and more susceptible to forest fires. These changes have the potential to transform alpine landscapes and their ability to sustain human settlements, as well as to affect recreational activities and tourism.

Switzerland's population has more than doubled from 3.3 million in 1900 to more than 8 million today. Some cities have expanded so significantly that they have merged together to create dense strips of human settlement along lakes. Urban and industrial expansion are continuing to **encroach** on an already limited amount of arable land. They are also putting mounting pressure on Switzerland's water sources.

CHAPTER 4 A Vibrant Country

What Makes Switzerland Special?

Switzerland is recognized internationally as a politically neutral country. This strategy dates back to the 16th century, when the Swiss Confederation was defeated by France in a regional conflict. To avoid future conflicts and protect its borders, Switzerland decided to assume neutral status. Several centuries later, Napoleon invaded Switzerland. Soon after he was defeated, European leaders decided that a neutral Switzerland could provide much-needed stability for the continent. In 1815, a declaration made Switzerland's neutrality official within the international community.

The position of neutrality has guided Switzerland through two World Wars in the 20th century, and more recent conflicts across the globe. It has cemented Switzerland's status as a country that honors stability, diplomacy, and peace over conflict and uncertainty. Switzerland has also become well known for its **humanitarian** and diplomatic efforts to work toward a world of peace and human rights for all. Geneva is the headquarters for many global organizations and NGOs, or nongovernmental organizations, such as the Red Cross, the United Nations, and Médecins Sans Frontières.

The United Nations, or UN, is an international organization of 193 countries. Its goal is to solve problems and meet goals that benefit the global community.

The highly regarded University of Basel, established in 1460, is rich in history and tradition.

Closer Look

Henry Dunant

Switzerland boasts an impressive list of Nobel Prize winners and global leaders in the arts and sciences. Henry Dunant is one of them. Deeply concerned about the European soldiers injured and killed in conflict during the 19th century, he laid out a plan for countries to help soldiers wounded on the battlefield. This led to the creation of the International Committee of the Red Cross (ICRC) in 1863. Soon after, the Geneva Convention was adopted. This document established international standards for humanitarian treatment of civilians and soldiers during conflict. Dunant was awarded the Nobel Peace Prize in 1901 for his work. The ICRC continues his legacy today and is a strong symbol of Switzerland's commitment to humanitarianism.

Henry Dunant

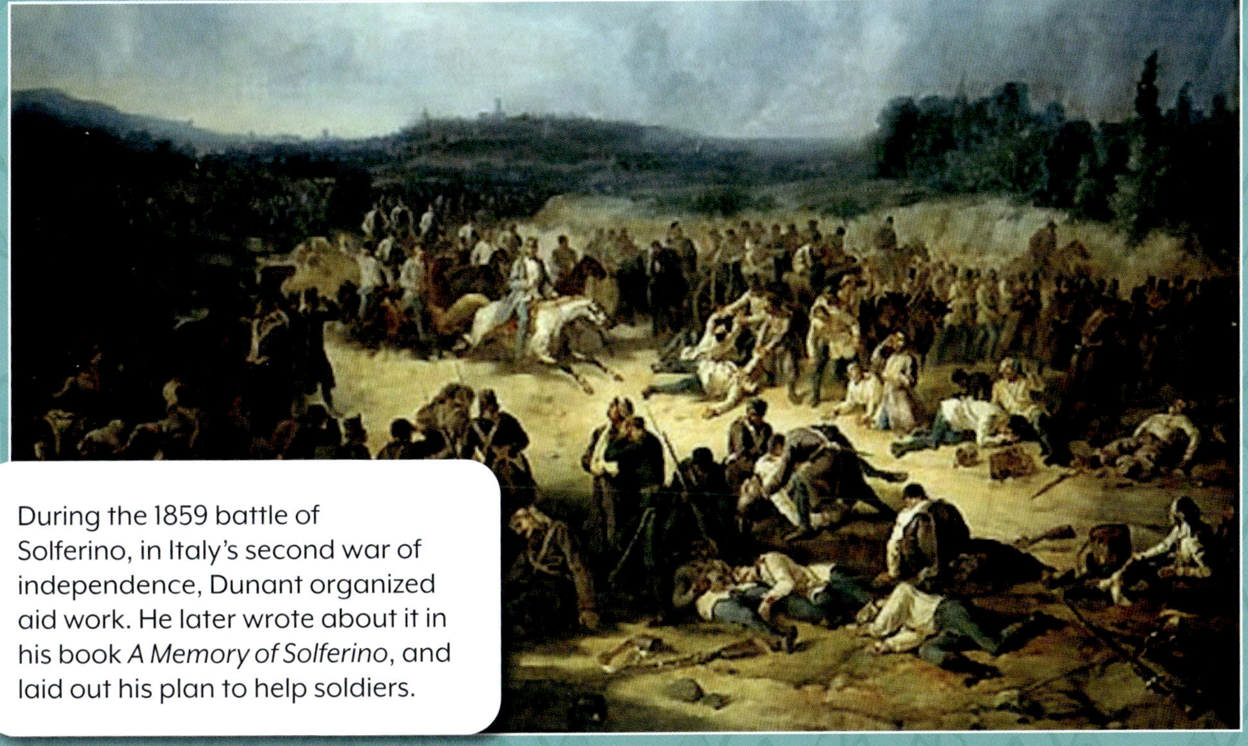

During the 1859 battle of Solferino, in Italy's second war of independence, Dunant organized aid work. He later wrote about it in his book *A Memory of Solferino*, and laid out his plan to help soldiers.

Festivals and Celebrations

Switzerland celebrates a number of ancient festivals and holidays. Many of these are rooted in the traditions of the country's religions, agriculture, and trade **guilds**. *Silvesterchläusen*—or Saint Sylvester's Day—celebrates the New Year and dates back to the times of Switzerland's medieval **monasteries**. During this holiday, performers wander from house to house, ringing bells and yodeling New Year's wishes. They wear costumes which incorporate natural elements such as twigs, ivy, grasses, and moss. This tradition is practiced in the canton of Appenzell.

Sechseläuten means "six-o-clock bell ringing." It is an annual tradition to announce the beginning of spring and is rooted in the culture of Switzerland's historic guilds. Before electricity was invented, guildsmen, or craftsmen, could only work until sunset. In winter, this happened around five o'clock in the afternoon. But with longer daylight hours in springtime, they could work for one hour longer. So on the first day of spring, the town's church bells would ring at six o'clock. Today the tradition is celebrated in Zürich.

Elaborate headpieces or fierce-looking masks often complete the *Silvesterchläuse* costumes.

Spring in Zürich is also marked by the parade of the guilds, which precedes the burning of the *Böögg*.

Spring is also celebrated in Zürich with the burning of the *Böögg*. A large woodpile is built in the town square and is topped with a snowman whose head is stuffed with straw, cotton, and explosives. Townspeople dress in the costumes of their traditional guilds—bakers, butchers, carpenters, and others—and gather in the town square to watch the ceremony. As the fire is lit and spreads from the woodpile to the snowman, they wait for his head to explode, signifying that the end of winter is coming soon.

Alpabzug, or Alpine Cow Descent, reflects Switzerland's agricultural heritage. Each fall, before snow blankets the mountainsides, farmers bring their cattle down from the mountain pastures to spend the winter in the villages. To mark this occasion, the cows are decorated with flowery headdresses and large bells around their necks. These can be heard from miles away. Farmers dress in traditional costumes and villagers mark the occasion with music, market stalls, and delicious local foods.

Alpine Cow Descents take place throughout Switzerland in September, before the first frosts hit at the high altitudes.

Schwingen, or Swiss wrestling, is also a popular sport in Switzerland. Wrestlers wear belts that are held by their opponents.

Sports, Music, and Food

While skiing is Switzerland's official national sport, other traditional sports are also popular. *Hornussen* is a sport that dates back centuries. Its name comes from the German word for "hornet." It is a blend of golf, baseball, and discus. The puck makes a buzzing sound—like an angry hornet—when it is hit. Points are awarded for the distance the puck travels. The opponents' goal is to prevent the puck from landing.

Yodeling began as a way to communicate between isolated alpine communities before there were telephones or the Internet. Farmers also yodeled to call their cattle. Today yodeling is often performed at regional festivals. Its style varies across different regions.

The alphorn (see page 37) is a uniquely shaped instrument, traditionally carved from one piece of red pine that is longer than a person is tall. Like yodeling, it may once have been used to communicate between villages.

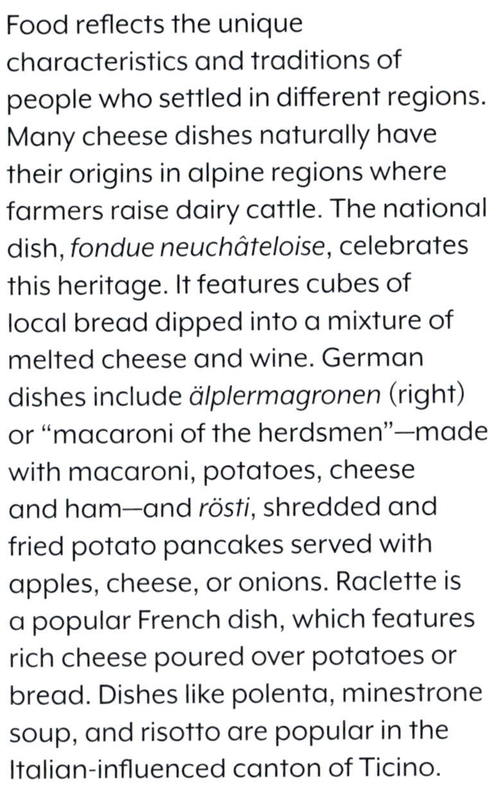

Food reflects the unique characteristics and traditions of people who settled in different regions. Many cheese dishes naturally have their origins in alpine regions where farmers raise dairy cattle. The national dish, *fondue neuchâteloise*, celebrates this heritage. It features cubes of local bread dipped into a mixture of melted cheese and wine. German dishes include *älplermagronen* (right) or "macaroni of the herdsmen"—made with macaroni, potatoes, cheese and ham—and *rösti*, shredded and fried potato pancakes served with apples, cheese, or onions. Raclette is a popular French dish, which features rich cheese poured over potatoes or bread. Dishes like polenta, minestrone soup, and risotto are popular in the Italian-influenced canton of Ticino.

Fondue (above) was traditionally enjoyed by alpine families, who made it from the milk of the family cows.

Älplermagronen

A popular alphorn song, the *Ranz des Vaches*, celebrates the season when cows are taken up to their summertime alpine pastures.

Religion and Culture

Along with the languages and cultures brought to Switzerland by people from other places, religion has also helped shape the country. Christianity arrived in Switzerland with Roman soldiers in the 4th century. The original three cantons of the Swiss Confederation were Roman Catholic. They held strongly conservative and traditional values.

As refugees fled religious wars in other parts of Europe in the 16th century, they brought Protestant Christianity to Switzerland. Their values of wisdom and hard work were quickly adopted in the wealthier rural cantons and cities that made up the heartland of Switzerland's industrial and agricultural activities. They were instrumental in helping draft the constitution in 1848 and its system to support the country's growing industrial economy. Geneva, in particular, was a safe haven for Protestant refugees fleeing **oppression**. They made an important contribution to the city's wealth, economy, and culture, which still survives today.

The Kapellbrücke, or Chapel Bridge, in Lucerne is famous for its paintings that date back to the 16th century. Named after the nearby St. Peter's Chapel, it is the oldest wooden covered bridge in Europe.

Chinigrossli celebrates the Christian holiday of the Epiphany, or Three Kings Day. Young people representing the three kings parade while wearing crowns and carrying decorated wooden horses.

These dancers celebrate Thai culture at a festival in Geneva.

More recently, Switzerland has seen the arrival of refugees fleeing violence from Eastern Europe, Asia, and Africa. These new arrivals continue to influence the country's culture, traditions, values, religion, and language. Islam, for example, has become the country's third-largest religion. As the religious and cultural makeup of Switzerland continues to shift, the rights **enshrined** in its constitution will help the country to embrace its unique brand of diversity and multiculturalism.

As the cultural makeup of Switzerland shifts, some traditions, languages, and values could be lost even as new ones are adopted. The mostly rural Lötschental Valley is home to ancient traditions such as *Chinigrossli*, a religious celebration that includes processions, feasts, and music. As some citizens move away from religion and rural life, these traditions and others like it are at risk of disappearing. There are similar fears about the Romansh language, which is spoken by fewer than 100,000 people in Switzerland today.

CHAPTER 5

Looking to the Future

Protecting Switzerland's Natural Environment

Growing 20th-century industry, agriculture, tourism, and human populations put enormous pressure on Switzerland's environment and natural resources. In the 1970s and 1980s, the Swiss government began to work with communities and industries to address concerns about acid rain, water pollution, and deforestation. Changes were made to encourage more **sustainable** agricultural practices.

In recent years, policies have been focused on preventing further environmental damage. Many cantons have created programs designed specifically to protect their natural environments and address regional issues. Each has a strong interest in protecting the unique natural beauty and lifestyles of their region for the sake of generations to come. On several issues, Switzerland tries to cooperate with the European Union (EU) to create and enforce environmental policies.

Protecting rivers and lakes is an important goal of the Swiss government. One method is adding extra treatment to wastewater to lessen pollution.

One key collaboration between Switzerland and the European Union is the pledge to reduce **greenhouse gas** emissions.

Closer Look

Environmental Strategies for the Future

Wildlife overpasses can help **reunify** habitats and allow safe passage for animals across roadways.

Switzerland's magnificent natural environment is a vital part of the country's character. To protect it, the government has adopted a number of measures. The key building blocks of its environmental strategy include the following goals:

1. To create an economy which encourages the development of sustainable products and behaviors by its citizens.
2. To encourage strategies which carefully manage the spread of urban development.
3. To fight climate change using fossil fuel taxes to help fund renewable energy programs.
4. To preserve the country's water quality by reducing the use of agricultural pesticides and improving wastewater treatment systems.
5. To encourage land use that supports wildlife and nature conservation.
6. To support the development of technologies to improve air quality.
7. To ensure that the country's landscapes are developed in a sustainable manner as healthy places to live, work, and play.

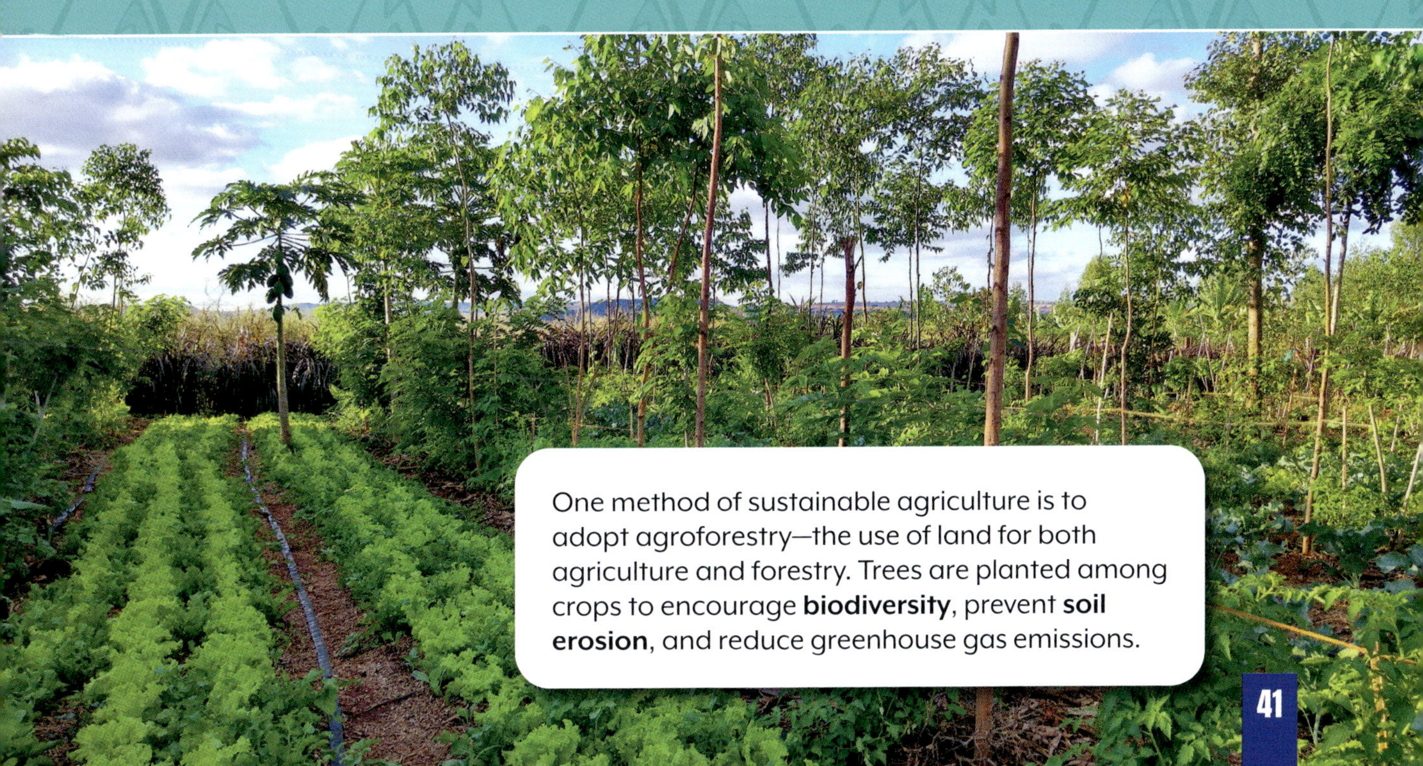

One method of sustainable agriculture is to adopt agroforestry—the use of land for both agriculture and forestry. Trees are planted among crops to encourage **biodiversity**, prevent **soil erosion**, and reduce greenhouse gas emissions.

At the Crossroads of Europe

The Swiss have always taken pride in being a self-determining nation able to create policies that are independent of its European neighbors. But balancing the will of the Swiss people against their country's commitment to international policies and laws can be difficult. Policies regarding migration, trade, and the environment are often issues that require the cross-border cooperation of many countries. European politicians point out that some initiatives approved by Swiss citizens in some cantons violate European law and economic policy. On the other hand, some Swiss politicians feel that the will of their people must be respected regardless of broader European policy.

Switzerland's constitution is unique in the amount of decision-making power given to citizens. The Swiss often vote on new laws and reforms in referendums.

The European Union is Switzerland's largest trading partner.

Economic trade is one issue that pits the will of the Swiss against international goals. In 1972, Switzerland negotiated a free-trade agreement with the European Economic Community. This allowed the Swiss to participate in a system which allows goods and people to flow freely across Europe. It gave the Swiss access to a much larger market to which they could sell their goods. But the Swiss have been reluctant to fully integrate their economy with the European Union. Switzerland's insistence on setting its own policies to guide its trading relationships has sometimes been a source of frustration to its EU partners.

Immigration is another important issue for Switzerland. Some Swiss people want to limit immigration because they feel it contributes to a high cost of living or loss of traditional culture. Switzerland's low birth rates and aging population, however, mean its population is declining. Immigration is essential to guarantee enough people to support its industry and economy. Switzerland's share of immigrants within its population is one of the highest in the world. Many new immigrants are young, highly educated, and bring important skills in technology, health care, and finance.

Immigration is essential for Switzerland's economic growth.

Managing Urban Development

Switzerland's population is expected to grow to 10.4 million by 2050. With limited space to expand cities, agriculture, and industry, the Swiss government will need strategies to manage the country's environment sustainably. At the same time, it will need to maintain the high quality of life expected by Swiss citizens. More people mean larger cities and the potential for further **urban sprawl** along its lakes and into its countryside. In recent decades, urban sprawl has been a characteristic of Switzerland's larger cities. Most often, this expansion comes at the cost of precious agricultural land.

Agriculture and farming represent some of the largest uses of land in Switzerland. In the more fertile areas of the central plateau and southern Jura Mountains, more than half of the land is dedicated to agriculture. With much of the country's citizens also based there, this means constant competition for available land. A recent study found that between 1985 and 2009, agricultural land in the country shrank at a rate of 11.8 square feet (1.1 sq. m) per second. If this loss continues, there will be serious consequences for Switzerland's agricultural future.

One goal is to limit urban sprawl by developing inward—using existing urban space more effectively to avoid developing untouched land.

Currently Switzerland's land use is divided, with approximately one-third dedicated to agriculture; one-tenth to urban areas; one-third to forests; and one-quarter designated as "unproductive" land. This is land covered in lakes, glaciers, or mountains. It is not useful for urban development, industry, or agriculture. However, this "unproductive" land is an important part of Switzerland's environmental heritage and natural beauty. To protect its biodiversity and landscapes, Switzerland has designated almost one-quarter of its lands as sites of national importance. These are important in sustaining people in other ways—such as tourism, recreation, and a vital supply of water. They will be an important part of Switzerland's land-use strategy as the 21st century evolves.

Red fox

Protecting the natural environment helps to protect biodiversity. With almost half of Switzerland's habitat types threatened, the country is creating protected areas for plant and animal species.

Marmots

Initiatives to protect soil can help protect Switzerland's fertile agricultural land. One method is to develop a plan to rotate crops to avoid soil **degradation**.

acid rain Any type of precipitation that is unusually acidic. Most acid rain is caused by burning fossil fuels.

arable Land that is fit for growing crops

biodiversity Variety of living things in an area

canton A small political region of a country

commercial Concerned with buying and selling

conifers Trees and shrubs that bear their seeds in cones. Most conifers have needles or scale-shaped leaves that they keep all year.

consolidate To join together to make a stronger whole

currents Bodies of water or air that move in a certain direction

deciduous Trees or shrubs that shed or lose their leaves each year

diplomacy The practice of managing relationships and negotiations between countries

encroach To intrude on

enshrined Preserved in a form that gives protection and respect

epicenter The central point

fertile Land on which plants can grow

feudal Referring to the social system of the Middle Ages, in which landowners allowed people to use their land in exchange for labor and loyalty

fortified Made stronger and more secure; added protective features

freight Goods transported in large quantities by train, ship, plane, or truck

greenhouse gas A gas, such as carbon dioxide, that traps heat in Earth's atmosphere

guilds Organizations of craftsmen or merchants, especially in medieval Europe

humanitarian Promoting human welfare

industrial Industry-based, focused on manufacturing goods

industrialized Changed from mostly agricultural to more industrial

inhospitable Difficult to live in; harsh

irrigated Supplied water to land so that plants and crops could grow

landlocked Completely, or almost completely, enclosed by land. Landlocked countries have no access to oceans.

medieval Related to the Middle Ages, the time period from approximately 500 to 1500

moderates Keeps within reasonable limits

monasteries Housing for communities of monks

Neanderthals An extinct species of human that lived around 30,000 to 200,000 years ago

neutral Impartial; not supporting a certain side during conflict

nomadic Moving from place to place

oppression Cruel or unjust treatment of a particular group by those in power, often governments

pharmaceutical Relating to medicinal drugs

plateau A large, mostly flat area at a higher elevation than surrounding land

population density A measurement of the number of people living within a certain area

precision machinery A process that uses advanced, computer-controlled machines to create products with high accuracy

profitable Making money

quaint Having old-fashioned or unusual charm

raw materials Natural resources or materials that have not been processed into finished goods

resins Thick substances produced by trees and other plants. Resins protect plants and can also be used to make a variety of products.

reunify Bring a divided group or area back together as one

soil degradation A decline in soil quality, making it less suitable for supporting agriculture or plant and animal life

soil erosion Gradual wearing away of top layers of soil

sparse Thinly scattered

sustainable Able to be used in a way that does not deplete natural resources or cause significant environmental damage

textiles Cloth or woven fabrics

topography The features in an area of land, such as mountains and rivers

UNESCO World Heritage Site A protected landmark or area singled out by the United Nations Educational, Scientific, and Cultural Organization (UNESCO) as being globally significant

urban sprawl The expansion of urban areas outward onto undeveloped land—often rapid and poorly planned

urbanized Changed from mostly rural to more urban, with more cities

watershed An area of land that drains, or sheds, water such as rivers and streams into a larger body of water

Books

Miles, John. *Pathways Through Europe*. Crabtree Publishing, 2020.

Ojha, Bandana. *Switzerland: 100+ Amazing & Interesting Facts You Didn't Know Before.* Independent, 2022.

Peppas, Lynn. *The Alps.* Crabtree Publishing, 2012.

Seavey, Lura Rogers. *Switzerland*. Scholastic Children's Press, 2016.

Websites

https://www.eda.admin.ch/aboutswitzerland/en/home.html
A comprehensive website on everything "Swiss" from the Swiss Confederation.

https://www.kids-world-travel-guide.com/switzerland-facts.html
A detailed look at Switzerland's geography, climate, people and culture, government, history, and economy.

https://kids.britannica.com/students/article/Bern/273189
Learn more about Switzerland's capital city and then follow links to explore other cities across the country.

https://www.ifrc.org
Learn more about the International Red Cross and Red Crescent Societies, which were founded in Switzerland.

About the Author

Linda Barghoorn has written thirty children's books for which she studied a wide range of topics, from deserts and earthquakes to refugees, resilient cities, and remarkable people. She is an avid learner, explorer, and traveler. When she's not at work, she can most often be found hiking or curled up with a good book.